MENTAL
IN MARTIAL ARTS
SKILLS

TO: Joy,

The Journey is the reward!

by

Miguel Hernández

2013

Published by WINNERS SPORTS ®
Brooklyn, New York

First Edition
First Printing • 1,000 • May 1997

Library of Congress Catalog Card Number: # 97-93556
ISBN 1-57502-447-0

FRONT COVER PHOTOGRAPH BY John Fitzgerald

Printed in the USA by

MP
MORRIS PUBLISHING

3212 East Highway 30 • Kearney, NE 68847 • 1-800-650-7888

Dedicated to the Moy Yat Ving Tsun Kung Fu Family who put themselves on the line daily in their quest for excellence.

CONTENTS

CHAPTER

1. TOTAL MARTIAL ARTIST   1

2. THE ULTIMATE COMPETITOR   3

3. THE IDEAL PERFORMANCE STATE   7

4. MENTAL TOUGHNESS   11

5. GOAL-SETTING: THE ROAD to SUCCESS   18

6. RELAXATION TRAINING   24

7. MENTAL CONTROL of EMOTIONS and STRESS   33

8. IMAGERY: USING the MIND to PROGRAM the BODY   43

9. CONCENTRATION   58

10. PERFORMANCE ROUTINE   64

1

TOTAL MARTIAL ARTIST

In 1991, I took a pioneering step in my development. Recognizing the importance of developing the total martial artist, including the practitioner's mental skills, I started to research psychological skills training programs as a formal part of my development programs, and such training was later introduced at the Ving Tsun Kung Fu Studio as well.

The program was designed to promote the learning of mental skills that can make the difference between success and failure in martial arts. Training in psychological skills such as goal-setting, concentration, relaxation, and mental rehearsal was incorporated into my training and martial arts.

This book has been developed as part of the psychological skills training program. It is designed to help you develop mental skills that can enhance your performance. It focuses on the strategies and skills that have always marked great martial artists and boxers. These skills were learned by me and many martial artists, during the course of their careers, often through trail and error. While it may be true that "experience is the best teacher," I believe that the "experience" can take many forms and that these skills can be learned early in a martial artist's journey through a structured training program like the one outlined in this book. My goal is to accelerate this learning process so as to give you the best chances of succeeding in your quest.

Confronted by the sobering fact that only about five percent of students who sign on ever reach the final stages of their martial art, you owe it to yourself to take advantage of every opportunity to learn and develop yourself both physically and mentally. As a kung fu instructor, I owe you the opportunity to maximize your abilities so that one day, hopefully, you may pass on these skills. This book and the program it comes from is intended to help you become the best martial artist you can be. Moreover, the skills you will learn in this book are also life skills that apply far beyond martial arts. They can help you be more successful in any walk of life, for martial arts are in many respects a microcosm of life.

As a coach, I am not satisfied only to develop a better martial artist; I also want my practitioners to become better people. It is my hope that what you learn from this book will benefit you in both respects--------as a martial artist and as a person.

2

THE ULTIMATE COMPETITOR

Most martial artists are already aware that there is more to competition than simply learning the physical skills of the art. This was brought home to me several years ago when I did a study involving all of the Moy Yat Ving Tsun Kung Fu students at New York City's Soho branch. Each practitioner was carefully rated on his physical skills by some senior student who knew him best. I rated technique speed and control, range and ability, movement and control of techniques, as well as other physical skills. Thus, for each practitioner, I had measures of his physical tools, obviously, martial artists differed from one another in their judged physical abilities.

I then prepared a measure of each students statistical performance that year. The practitioners also differed widely from one another in how well they performed. The question I was interested in was this: How much of the variation in performance could be accounted for by differences in physical skills?

When I correlated the *"physical tools"* and performance measures with others, I discovered a rather startling fact: Differences in physical ability accounted for only about 25 percent of the variation in actual performance. The other 75 percent of the difference was being caused by other factors?

I believe that the other factors were in large part psychological ones. It is one thing to possess the needed physical skills and quite another to be able to use them when it really counts. The five percent of martial artists who reach stardom and a still smaller percentage who stay there and have solid careers, are not necessarily the most physically talented practitioner. In many cases, they were overshadowed in the class by "*can't miss*" talent who had the tools to be potential superstars, yet never made it to the top because the gap between their abilities and their performance widened as the martial art got tougher. Those who make it to the top and stay there are the ones who are able to consistently apply their tools and perform near their upper performance range. They *Won* the battle with the ultimate competitor: Themselves. They have mastered the ultimate challenge: The challenge of self-control.

THE SEARCH FOR CONSISTENCY

Unless you are very unusual, you are no stranger to one of the greatest frustrations in martial arts: Inconsistency. Why do you play well one day, and less well the next day? How can you perform at an outstanding level for a period of time, then perform, miserably and drop into a slump? Are there times when you feel as if you're playing Russian Roulette with yourself when you go to class, not knowing if you're going to have a good outing or a poor one?

There are few things so frustrating to a martial artist as the knowledge that you are not performing up to your ability. How can you have such great moves while playing the forms, then lose it all in a sparring session. How can you take or miss punches you should be smoking? Why do you tighten up or lose your concentration under pressure and fail to make that easy technique? Questions like these can be powerful triggers of guilt, self-doubt, anger, and self-criticism. Some practitioners find these feeling so painful that continuing in martial arts is not worth it, and they walk away from their dream. Many others continue to struggle, but fail to get either the enjoyment or performance that they know they are capable of.

4

How does one achieve the ability to perform consistently to ones potential? Such consistency is the earmark of any real master, and it requires two things. The first is good technique and form. If your fundamentals are poor, you are going to perform inconsistently regardless of your physical talent or mental toughness.

The second requirement for consistent performance is a mental makeup that allows you to be consistent psychologically. As you will come to see, playing consistently well is the result of creating a particular state of mind and body. This occurs as you achieve self-control over the mind-body connection.

THE ULTIMATE CHALLENGE

In a very real sense your ultimate competition is with yourself. You have been given a great deal of physical talent or you would not be a martial artist. But physical talent is not enough. The key to your success is to take the potential you have and develop it. No one else can do it for you, and no one can keep you from doing it for yourself. While there are many circumstances in martial arts that you cannot control, the one thing you can learn to control is yourself. You can control your thoughts, your emotions, your effort, and the strategies you use to get better, failure to do so will place you at the mercy of the situations in which you find yourself and will breed inconsistency and an inability to achieve your potential. In this sense, you will always be your toughest opponent. If you have the needed talent, the greatest obstacle between you and your goal is you.

A SUCCESS FORMULA

Winning the contest with yourself is hard work. It takes commitment on your part to become the best that you can be and pay whatever price is necessary to win that contest with yourself.

This commitment must be expressed everyday in your work habits and in the effort you expend. Thus the first step in self-mastering is _self-discipline._

Self-discipline leads to self-control, for it helps you do what is necessary to gain greater control of your thoughts, emotions, and behavior. Without self-control you will never reach your true potential as a martial artist or as a person.

Self-control leads directly to an increase in self-confidence, for the best form of self confidence comes from knowing that you are in control of yourself and that you have prepared yourself as well as you can. With that belief in place, you can perform with abandon and let the chips fall where they may.

Self-discipline, self-control, and self-confidence are powerful tools for self-realization, being the best that you are capable of being. I would emphasize the importance of striving to be not the best (which may be beyond the reach of your physical capabilities), but your best. No one is capable of more.

All of the techniques in this book are intended to help you increase your self-discipline, self-control, self-confidence and self-realization. As you will see, the concept of mental toughness does not refer to an inborn quality that people either have or do not have. Instead, mental toughness is a set of specific psychological skills that can be learned. Once learned these skills make possible the self-control and performance consistency that marks "_mentally tough_" martial artists and allows them to achieve peak performance under the most demanding pressure conditions. These skills allow you to put yourself more consistently in the ideal performance state, a state of mind and body that is associated with peak performance. Let us, therefore, examine the nature of this special state!

3

THE IDEAL PERFORMANCE STATE

A state is a condition of mind and body. We are always in one state or another and our state can change from one moment to another. To illustrate the concept of a state, lets try a quick exercise:

I would like you to recall and relive in as much detail as possible your finest hour as a martial artist, a time when you performed at your absolute peak. Imagine the details of the situation and try to recapture the thoughts and feelings you experienced at that moment.

When you have succeeded in recapturing that experience, indicate how you felt at that point in time:

1. Muscles Relaxed	1 2 3 4 5	Muscles Tight
2. Calm & Quiet	1 2 3 4 5	Fast &Frantic
3. Low Anxiety	1 2 3 4 5	High Anxiety
4. High Energy	1 2 3 4 5	Low Energy
5. Positive	1 2 3 4 5	Negative
6. Highly Enjoyable	1 2 3 4 5	Unenjoyable
7. Effortless	1 2 3 4 5	Great Effort
8. Automatic	1 2 3 4 5	Deliberate
9. Confident	1 2 3 4 5	Not Confident
10.Alert	1 2 3 4 5	Dull
11.In Control	1 2 3 4 5	Out of control
12.Focused	1 2 3 4 5	Unfocused
13.Played Well	1 2 3 4 5	Played Poorly
14.Positive Energy	1 2 3 4 5	Negative Energy

MENTAL SKILLS

The terms in the scales you just completed come from research studies by Doctors Jim Loeher, Ken Ravzza, and Charles Garfeild in which hundreds of athletes were asked to describe their peak performance experiences in their own words. Although different methods of interviewing were used, the results of these studies paint a consistent portrait of what the ideal performance state should be like.

Basically, the athletes tended to describe their ideal body-mind state in the terms on the left side of the scales. Is this pattern consistent with your ratings of your experience?

Let us examine the characteristics of this state in greater detail.

1. Physically Relaxed. Athletes most often reported that their muscles felt loose and relaxed and their movements fluid and sure.
2. Mentally Relaxed. They described their state as one of internal calm. Some also reported a sense of time slowing down and their being able to concentrate almost totally on whatever they needed to. By contrast, losses in concentration were associated with a sense of everything happening too fast and being out of control.
3. Confident and Optimistic. Athletes felt a sense of great self confidence and optimism. They felt able to maintain poise and control even under the most challenging situations.
4. Highly Energized. They felt pumped with a positive energy that was quite different from anxiety, fear, anger, or frustration. They were "pumped" and "charged" with something that was almost joyful, but yet, they felt a profound sense of inner calmness and control.
5. Effortless and Automatic. They didn't have to force anything. Their bodies and minds reacted to effortless and seemingly "involuntary" manner, as if they were on "automatic pilot". They sense that they could let go and let their skills and reflexes simply take over. Rather than "trying harder" they tried "softer" and went with the flow".
6. Self-Confident. Most of the practitioners reported a sense of being at the top of their skill level and knowing they were going to

perform to their capabilities. They were less concerned with the possibility of failure and more in tune with enjoying their performance.

7.Great Awareness. Many of the athletes reported an extraordinary sense of awareness of their own bodies and of what was going on around them. They seemed to know what the other practitioners were going to do and found themselves reacting quickly and automatically. Some reported being in a "cocoon" in which they had complete access to all their powers and skills.

8. In Control. All of the above characteristics resulted in a feeling of extraordinary control over body and mind. The athletes could maintain both their focus and relaxed intensity and they enjoyed the sense of "getting it all together".

Understanding your state of mind is the key to understanding change and achieving excellence. If I were to ask you to recall your worst moment in martial arts, a time when you performed miserably or gave in to pressure instead of peaking, chances are your ratings would be more over to the right side of the scales. We always do the best we can under the circumstances, but sometimes we find ourselves in unresourceful states that prevent us from performing to our ability.

Most of our state of mind happen without any conscious direction on our part. We see or hear something and go into a state. It may be a resourceful state like the ideal performance state, or it may be an unresourceful state of tension, distraction, and loss of confidence that defeats our performance. But it need not be this way. One important difference between ideal performers and those who are not is that the elite performers have learned how to consistently put themselves in a state that supports them in their achievements.

There are two major components to a state, one having to do with body, the other with mind. The first is our physiology, that is how the body is reacting. Thus, a state of anxiety involves muscle tension, butterflies in the stomach, a pounding heart, and other ways that our body prepares for avoiding a threat to its well-being. The mental part of anxiety involves worry, loss of concentration, intruding thoughts about our inability to deal with the situation, and so on. If you look at the characteristics of the ideal performance state, you will see that some of them reflect physiology, others involve mental events, and some reflect both components ("For example, the effortless and automatic feelings of flow").

Mind and body are inseparable, and they constantly interact to form our states. The states, in turn influence the type of behavior we produce. Thus to control and direct our behaviors we must be able to direct and consciously control our thoughts and physiology. That is the great hope of mental training. Either we can wait and hope that an ideal performance state will occur just when we need it, or we can learn specific skills that will enable us to produce the state and stay in it more consistently.

Our performance can vary a great deal, but our physical skills do not go up and down like a yo-yo. We don't suddenly forget how to throw a punch or a kick from one day to the next. We are not strong one minute and weak the next. What changes is our state, not our skill, and if we want to perform more consistently, then we must learn how to get ourselves into the ideal performance state more often, and how to stay there when adversity causes us to begin losing it. That's what the *Martial Arts* mental toughness training program is designed to teach you. Let us, then consider the nature of mental toughness and what can be done to increase it.

4

MENTAL TOUGHNESS

One of the finest compliments any martial artist can receive is to be called "mentally tough". Probably the two greatest attributes that a martial artist can have are physical talent and mental toughness. These two characteristics combine to create a *"total martial artist"* who is tough to beat.

Mental toughness is the key to consistency that all martial artists seek in their peak performance. The physical talent we have does not change much from day to day, week to week, or month to month. What can fluctuate a great deal is the mind-body state that martial artists bring to competition with them. The key to a consistent top performance is the ability to create the ideal performance state in yourself. So that your mental game is as constant as your physical abilities.

What is this characteristic of mental toughness? A good standing point is to say what it is *not*. It is not some inborn quality that people either have or do not have. Rather, it is a set of behaviors, or abilities, that permit martial artists to remain close to their ideal performance state even under the most adverse conditions. In many ways, the mentally tough martial artist is opposite of the martial artist who chokes under pressure or quits under adversity.

MENTAL SKILLS

WHAT IS MENTAL TOUGHNESS?

I've asked a great many masters, coaches, and top martial artists in many styles what the characteristics of the mentally tough martial artists are. There is great consistency in their responses. When I ask them, "what is it that mentally tough martial artists **do** that separates them from other martial artists?" Here are the characteristics they describe:

1.*Emotional control in the face of adversity*

The hallmark of a mentally tough martial artist is his ability to maintain poise, concentration, and emotional control under the most demanding of conditions. When other martial artists are falling apart or choking, the mentally tough martial artist is reaching down inside and remaining cool and collected under fire. Bad calls by the referees, stupid mistakes by classmates, obnoxious opponents, poor training conditions all represent powerful triggers for negative emotions. However, mentally tough martial artists can control anger, frustration, and fear so that these emotions do not control them.

2.*Ability to Concentrate under Distraction and Pressure*

We all know how difficult it can be to remain focused under pressure and adversity. It is too easy to become distracted and lose concentration when opponents are fighting you, onlookers are screaming at you, and self doubt is creeping into your mind. Under such conditions, a mentally tough martial artist is able to tune in what's important and tune out what is not. For long periods of time, they are able to focus their attention completely on the task at hand, the job that needs to be done. This quality is especially important in martial arts, where concentration is so critical to a good performance. When practitioners begin to respond to pressure *situations* with pressure responses, one of the first things to go is their concentration.

3. *View pressure situations as challenges and opportunities*

Mentally tough martial artists do not avoid pressure situations or regard pressure situations as threats. Rather, they are challenged by such situations and see them as another opportunity to test themselves and to explore the limits of their potential. Mentally tough martial artists want to be in the fight when the title is on the line. They want to be the one to throw the crucial punch. They want the kick to be thrusted at them when the fight is on the line. These are all opportunities for them to put their mind, body, and emotions on the line.

4.*Peaks Under Pressure*

The foregoing characteristics help bring about perhaps the most remarkable characteristics of the mentally tough martial artist: the ability to peak under pressure. Emotional control, focus on the task at hand, and viewing pressure situation as challenges and opportunities causes mentally tough martial artists to perform at their best when the chips are down. Not only is their performance better, but they also take advantage of the fact that their opponents begin to tighten up and perform poorly under pressure. All of the truly great competitors have had this quality of performing at their best under pressure, and this is the true mark of the mentally tough martial artist.

5.*Optimistic & self-confident*

Mentally tough martial artists have an air of self-confidence. They seem to know that when the chips are down, they're going to perform at their best. It seems nearly impossible to shatter their confidence and belief in themselves and in their ability to perform well. They almost never fall victim to self-defeating thoughts and ideas, and as a consequence, they are not easily intimidated. On the contrary, because of their confident appearance, they can be intimidating without ever opening their mouths. When the chips are down, classmates know that they can depend on these martial artists.

6.Self-Motivated and directed

Mentally tough martial artists have great self-discipline and self-direction. They are "self-starters" who don't have to be pushed to pay the price for excellence. They never miss an opportunity to practice and get better. A good example of self-motivation was Bruce Lee. Though perhaps the greatest martial artist of his time, Lee threw hundreds of punches every day from the time he was a teenager to the day he died. He knew what he had to do to get to the top of his form and stay there, and he took charge of himself and his career. The self-directed martial artist is often the first to the kung fu studio and the last to leave, even in the dog days of August. He gains an inner strength from taking charge of himself.

Mentally tough martial artists take full responsibility for their own actions. There are no excuses. They know they did their best, and that they either did or didn't get the job done. Ultimately, everything begins and ends with them, and they are perfectly comfortable with that and fully aware that their testing as a martial artist is in his or her own hands.

7.Consistency in performance

As noted earlier, consistency is one of the hallmarks of the mentally tough martial artist. Because they exercise the self-control needed to remain mentally focused and emotionally controlled, their performance varies less than is the case for many other martial artists.

Practitioners who have the characteristics of mental toughness dominate the world of martial arts. The world's greatest boxers provide testimony to the reality of mental toughness every time they perform. They have a special kind of inner strength, a strength that goes beyond the limits of their natural talent and skills. At the elite levels of martial arts, difference in physical talent are often minimal and it can be a very thin line that separates those who succeed from those who do not. Boxing coach immortal Ray Arcel recognized this fact when he said, "A fighter must learn to think, think, and think."

Mental Toughness as Psychological skills

Mental toughness is not a quality that we are born with. It is not a competitive instinct that comes to us in our genes. Instead, mental toughness is a set of psychological skills that are learned. If you are a mentally tough competitor, you've learned it through your life experience. If you're not mentally tough, you haven't learned it yet. The process through which mental toughness is acquired is precisely the same as that which applies to developing physical skills: understanding, hard work, and practice. In other words if you want to be mentally tougher, you can be. This book will show you how.

Mental toughness consists of the skills that are needed to maintain control over the ideal performance state. As we saw earlier, this state enhances performance, and martial artists who are able to produce it in themselves are more consistent in performing at the upper range of their talents and skills.

The *Martial Arts* psychological skills training program concentrates on a number of the master skills that constitute mental toughness. These skills include the following:

1. Goal Setting
2. Stress Management
3. Mental Rehearsal
4. Concentration
5. Performance Routines

These five sets of skills relate very specifically to the mentally tough competitor. Goal setting (chapter 5) is a key to self-discipline, self-direction, and internal motivation. In fact, goal setting is the most effective motivational technique known to psychology. It teaches you to define your goals very precisely and to develop action plans to achieve those goals. It puts you squarely in control of your own progress and development.

Stress management training (chapters 6&7) will teach you a set of mental and physical skills that increase your emotional self-control. You will learn how to physically relax your mind so as to replace self-defeating thought patterns with those that characterize the thinking of a mentally tough martial artist.

Mental rehearsal, or imagery (chapter 8) is a powerful technique for programming your mind and body to perform the behaviors that you wish to perform. As we shall see, research has shown that mental practice can result in significant performance improvement. Many great martial artists use mental rehearsal as part of their approach to their style.

Concentration (chapter 9) is an essential skill for *Ving Tsun Kung Fu* or any other martial arts. You will learn some effective ways of increasing your powers of concentration and your ability to focus your attention more effectively while playing martial arts.

Finally, in chapter 10, you will learn how to develop performance routines that allow you to incorporate the psychological skills you have learned into a success chain. With practice, these performance rituals can become powerful triggers for creating the ideal performance state. They help deepen concentration, raising or lowering intensity, staying loose, turning on the automatic, and other aspects of the ideal performance state. Most great performers in various professions or sports have developed mental and physical rituals to help them get ready to perform and to keep them in their ideal performance state. You will learn how to incorporate the skills you learn into a ritual that will become automatic with time and practice and will assist you in performing more effectively.

Assumptions Underlying Psychological Skills Training

Several assumptions about human behavior underlie psychological skills training. One starting assumption is that any given point in their lives, people do things the best way they know previous life experiences allow you to be. You are doing the very best that you can, given your present skills and knowledge and your past life experiences.

A second assumption is that you have the potential for much more. Most people don't know how to release their own potential but they can learn. In many ways, becoming the best you can be requires that you get out of your own way. Learning the psychological skills that compromise mental toughness can help you overcome many of your current limitations.

Another major assumption is that the mind and the body interact in both positive and negative ways. The mind affects the body, and the body affects the mind. Where the mind is concerned, the ways we think and the attitudes we cultivate makes a crucial difference in how we perform. What goes on inside the head can either enhance your performance or limit it.

A final assumption is that you are largely what you make of yourself. It is important that you take responsibility for yourself and your own personal development. It is your art, and you have the power to alter its course in either positive or negative ways. At the present time, you are doing the very best that you are capable of doing. But you can do better, and you will probably have to do better in order obtain your goals in martial arts. A dedication to becoming the very best that you can be certainly should involve the learning of mental toughness skills. These can help you not only to be a better martial artist, but also to be a more effective person. These psychological skills are powerful performance enhancers, but they are more than that. They are also life skills that will help you be a stronger and more effective person in other areas of your life both during and after your martial arts. These skills are not difficult to learn, but they require dedication and practice on your part. Considering the benefits that these skills can provide, they are well worth the effort.

5

Goal-Setting: The Road to Success

The same principle applies to you. Your future success as a martial artist depends in large part on your willingness to commit yourself to the goal of becoming the best you can be, both physically and mentally. Everything in this book is designed to help you work toward developing the mental skills that are needed to consistently perform at your best. In other words, each part of this book is a step-by-step approach to achieving a particular goal: a master skill.

Goal-setting, done correctly, is the most powerful tool for personal development that we know of. Winners in life have usually mastered the skill of setting challenging yet realistic goals, figuring out what they have to do on a day-by-day basis to achieve them, and making the commitment to do what is required. As they achieve each goal they set, they become more skillful, grow in self-confidence, and move ever closer to their future dream.

Why is systematic goal-setting so effective? There are several reasons:
1. Goals direct our attention and effort in a useful direction.
2. Working toward a specific and challenging goal makes us work harder, longer, and more productively.

3. Working toward a specific goal often helps us develop new and more effective ways to get there. Winners are always looking for a "better way" to achieve their performance goals.

4. Working toward and achieving specific goals increases our feelings of personal control and our self-confidence.

Goal-Setting and self-confidence

This last point is important, because all of us know how important confidence is to success in martial arts. But where does confidence come from? Certainly, it comes from success, and we all feel confident when things are going well. But the mentally tough martial artist keeps his confidence level up even when things are going poorly. Why? Because an even more basic source of self-confidence is confidence in our ability to get better...The belief that we know how to gain the skills that we need to overcome our current shortcomings. The martial artist who doesn't know how to get better feels helpless, hopeless, and full of self-doubt. The self-confident martial artist knows that he will find a way to get the job done. Knowledge of correct goal-setting methods is the map that can help get you where you want to go. It's a key to martial arts.

Keys to Effective Goal-setting

Perhaps you've noticed the emphasis on correct methods of goal-setting. As with any other skill in martial arts--punching, kicking, footwork--we know that some goal-setting approaches are more effective than others. There are some do's and don'ts.

To illustrate, let's do some goal-setting exercises right now.

1. First, write down your ultimate goals in martial arts.
   What would you like to achieve during your training?
   What is your dream? Use the space below.

2. Next, what are your goals for this year? List in specific terms exactly what you would like to accomplish.

Let's stop here for a moment. You've listed a number of long and short term goals. These goals can be further categorized: outcome goals and performance goals. Outcome goals are the end products of achievements, such as winning a competition, making the national team, or becoming a champion. They are the outcomes we try to achieve.

Performance goals have to do with the specific behaviors you need to master in order to achieve these outcomes. Examples of performance goals are distance awareness, movement-time, coordination of techniques, staying focused and alert on every move. Performance goals are the stepping stone to achieving outcome goals. They are the mechanical and mental things we need to do in order to achieve the outcomes we want.

Look back at the goals you've listed above. Are they outcome or performance goals? Chances are, many if not all of them are outcomes you want to achieve rather than specific behaviors you need to perform well in order to get there. Now, outcome goals are fine, for they help motivate and guide you. On the other hand, if you want to increase your chances of attaining them, you have to concentrate on what, specifically, you have to do today, tomorrow, and next week to achieve your outcome goals. In other words, you have to focus on your performance goals.

Effective goal-setting is like a staircase. You start at the bottom and proceed step by step to the top. The key to setting up the goal staircase is to be able to honestly and accurately identify the specific things you have to improve upon and to set up a reasonable action plan for achieving each step on the staircase. Then, you need to find a way to measure your progress at each step. The goals should be difficult and challenging, both to challenge you and give you a feeling of accomplishment when you attain them. Also, you should feel free to modify both the goals and the plan of action, if needed.

With these points in mind, let's return to your goal-setting exercise.
3. Look back at your goals. Now, ask yourself, "what are the specific things I need to do in order to achieve these goals?" What are the specific areas in which I need to improve?" These performance goals should take the form of specific behaviors that are keys to your getting better. List the specific goals below.

4. Now, list in order these goals from most important to least important and pick the top goal, the one you think you should work on first. Develop a specific action plan for improvement. Before doing so, however, consider these examples:
    A puncher who wanted to improve control of his accuracy decided that he will throw 100 punches each day. He and a fellow classmate kept count of punches on the target for the first few days and found that he was throwing about 40% of his punches in that area. The puncher then set the following goal: "In two weeks time, I want to be up to 50%." He continued his practice and his measurement of his "accuracy punch" to chart his performance.
    A kicker had a weakness with his right side kick and making a good thrust. By kicking at an air shield he tracked his successful kicks with the help of the instructor, he found he was at about 80%. He decided that he would do 50 kicks with his right leg each day, and that he would try to improve by 5% each week.
    There are several points worth noting here. First, the practitioners pinpointed the areas in which they wanted to improve. They then found a way to measure their current performance and keep track of changes in that specific behavior so they could chart improvement. One reason that charting performance is so important is that the improvements may be so slight that you wouldn't be aware of the real progress being made if you didn't have the numbers.
    Another point is very important. Both of the practitioners set challenging, but realistic goals. The puncher didn't set a goal of 100% on target. If he had, he'd set himself up for failure instead of

success. The goal of goal-setting is to feel good about the progress you're making.

Finally, the goals should be positive rather than negative ones. Always be focused on what you want to do rather than on what you want to avoid doing. This keeps you focused on success rather than on avoiding failure.

To summarize, goals should be:

(a) specific in nature

(b) challenging, but realistic

(c) short-term

(d) measurable on a day-to-day basis

(e) positive in nature

With these general guidelines in mind, go ahead and define your performance goal, indicate your action plan, and explain how you're going to measure your progress.

A. What is the specific performance goal? Make sure it is a behavior, not an outcome goal.

B. Spell out in detail your action plan. Exactly what are you going to do? When are you going to do it? What is the time span for attainment of the first step on the staircase?

C. How will you measure the specific performance you are working on?

As you are well aware, all the goals in the world do no good without the commitment to do whatever is necessary to attain them. The greats have been people willing to pay the price for excellence. As noted earlier, Bruce Lee punched a 1000 times a day from the time he began his Ving Tsun Kung Fu training until the end of his study of the system. Bruce Lee was legendary for his dedication to his conditioning and his work habits. But also important is the fact that his dedication and effort was channeled toward specific performance goals. On a day-to-day basis, the greats work on the things that are necessary to achieve their outcome goals.

A final point is important. Goal-setting is a performance-improvement strategy that can be applied to any area of your life. It can (and should) be used to attain the mental skills taught in this book as well as the physical skills needed to perform. Both sets of skills are necessary for optimal performance.

6

RELAXATION TRAINING
UNDERSTANDING YOUR BODY

In learning the skills that make you a total martial artist, you have gained exceptional control over the muscles of your body. You are capable of muscular movements that few people are able to master. Yet, some of that muscular control can suddenly vanish when you become tense, anxious, highly excited, or angry. These emotional states create increases in the activity of your body that physiologists term arousal. Thus, your heart begins to beat faster and harder, your breathing becomes shallower and faster and begins to occur high in your chest rather than in your stomach, and your muscles may become tense and tight. This natural response of the body to challenges and threats has sometimes been called the fight-or-flight response. It readies the body to confront demanding situations. How does this state of arousal affect performance?

Arousal and performance

A good deal of scientific research has been done to determine the relation between body arousal and skilled performance. This relation usually takes the form of an inverted-U, as shown in Figure 6.1. If we plot the level of body arousal on the horizontal axis of the graph and the performance on the vertical axis, we find that performance is poor when a player is underaroused or "flat." As arousal begins to increase, so does the performance curve, up to a certain point where performance is at its highest level. Beyond that optimal point, however, further increases in arousal begin to harm performance. At extremely high levels of arousal, performance may fall apart completely as the practitioner is "psyched out."

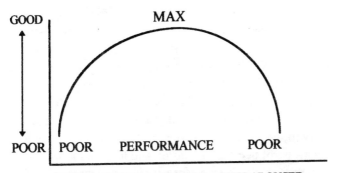

Figure 6.1 The arousal-performance relationship.

As noted when we considered the ideal performance state, most martial artists report that they are physically relaxed and loose when they are performing at their best. High levels of muscular tension can disrupt performance by reducing flexibility, muscular control, power, and speed of reaction. Because of delicate muscular control that is required to perform the complex skills of martial arts, high levels of muscular tension can have a devastating effect on performance. In addition, research has found that martial artists who are habitually tense are more prone to injury because their muscles are less flexible.

Mentally tough martial artists are able to maintain control of their level of arousal and keep it in the zone where their performance is best even under the most adverse conditions. This helps account for their consistency of performance and their ability to peak under pressure when less able martial artists are becoming tense and performing more poorly.

What Relaxation Training Can Do for you.

One of the most important skills any martial artist can learn is the ability to control arousal and to keep himself in the optimal performance zone. Because it is impossible to be relaxed and tense at the same time, relaxation skills are a highly effective way to combat emotional arousal that could harm performance; and they are essential stress management tool. A second benefit is that concentration becomes deeper and more focused when people are physically relaxed. Third, physical relaxation also increases the ability to tolerate pain (as you can prove to yourself next time you go to the dentist). Relaxation also increases the ability to use imagery or mental rehearsal; images are more vivid and controllable when mental rehearsal is done in a relaxed state. Finally, the process of learning the skill of relaxation will increase your sensitivity to what is occurring in your body. Thus, you will become more aware of developing tension and be able to turn it off before it can interfere with your performance. This increased body sensitivity will also help you to become more aware of what your muscles are doing and enable you to make quicker adjustments when you need to. For example, you may be able to quickly pick up a slight flaw in your kick or delivery and adjust on the next try.

It is important to note that relaxation is a skill. It involves voluntary control of the muscles just as kicking a heavy bag or a punch being thrust. Like other skills, it must be practiced in order for you to master it. Once learned, however, the ability to relax gives you a powerful level of command over your body.

Relaxation Techniques

In general, the techniques of relaxation can be divided into two categories, somatic relaxation and cognitive relaxation. Somatic (body) relaxation techniques are used to train the body to become sensitive to muscle tension and to be able to release or control muscle tension. This type of relaxation is extremely useful because it can quickly be applied in the performance situation to maintain control and keep you in your optimal physical state. With practice, you will be able to completely relax yourself within the space of one or two breathes, and you will be able to incorporate this skill into your performance routine.

The second form of relaxation is called cognitive (mental) relaxation. It is designed to clear the mind as well as to relax the body. This type of relaxation, learned through a simple meditation technique, is extremely useful as a general stress management technique, as a means of charging the body with new energy, and as a pre-workout technique for relaxing oneself.

We begin with somatic relaxation training, using a technique that involves learning to relax by tensing and relaxing the body. It also involves pairing your breathing and certain trigger words with the relaxed state so that they can serve as triggers for relaxation. This technique can quickly be learned by martial artists, who already have good control over their muscles. Within a week of practice, most practitioners can develop good relaxation skills.

Somatic Relaxation Training

This training technique is known as progressive muscle relaxation, and it has proven to be a highly effective technique to control muscle tension and general emotional arousal. The following procedure should allow you to begin to master this important self-control technique within a week or so. Once mastered, the relaxation response can be used to cope with stress or muscular tension in your body so that you can respond immediately to them.

It is recommended that the relaxation exercises be practiced at least twice a day until they are mastered. The exercises will initially require about 15 minutes of practice, but as you master the technique, the time required will become progressively shorter. Practice should be carried out in a comfortable chair, sofa, or bed (sitting up rather than lying down), and in a quiet atmosphere.

1. Get as comfortable as possible. tight clothing should be loosened and your legs should not be crossed. Take a deep breath, let it out slowly, and become as relaxed as possible. As you exhale, mentally say a word such as "relax," "loose," "calm," or some other

27

word that connotes relaxation to you. This is your "trigger word" that will become conditioned to the relaxed state through repeated association and will become capable of inducing relaxation as a result.

2. While sitting comfortably, bend your arms at the elbow. Now make a hard fist with both hands and bend your wrist downward while simultaneously tensing the muscle of your upper arms. This will produce a state of tension in your hands, forearms, and upper arms. Hold this tension for 5 seconds and study it carefully. Then slowly let the tension out halfway while concentrating on sensations in your arms and fingers as tension decreases. Hold the tension at the halfway point for 5 seconds, and then slowly let the tension out the rest of the way and let your arms rest comfortably in your lap. Concentrate carefully on the contrast between the tension you have just experienced and the relaxation which deepens as you voluntarily relax the muscles for an additional 10-15 seconds. As you breathe normally, concentrate on those muscles and say the trigger word (for example, "relax") to yourself each time you exhale. Do this for 7 to 10 breathes.

3. Tense the calf and thigh muscles in your legs . You can do this by straightening your legs out while at the same time pointing your toes downward. Hold the tension for 5 seconds, then slowly let it out halfway. Hold at the halfway point for an additional 5 seconds and slowly let the tension out all the way and concentrate on relaxing the muscles as completely as possible. Again, pay careful attention to the feelings of tension and relaxation as they develop. Finish by saying the trigger word each time you exhale (7 to 10 breaths) and concentrate on relaxing the leg muscle as deeply as possible.

4. Cross the palms of your hands in front of your chest and press them together so as to tense the chest and the shoulder muscles. At the same time, tense your stomach muscles. As before, hold the tension for 5 seconds, then slowly let the tension out all the way and concentrate on relaxing the muscles as completely as possible. Again, pay careful attention to the feelings of tension and release.

5. Arch your back and push your shoulders back as far as possible so as to tense your upper and lower back muscles. (Be careful not to tense these muscles too hard.) Repeat the standard procedure of slowly releasing the tension half way, then all the way. Finish by doing the breathing and trigger word as you deeply relax your back muscles.

6. Tense your neck and jaw muscles by thrusting your jaw outward and drawing the corners of your mouth back. Release the tension slowly to the halfway point, hold for 5 seconds, and then slowly release the tension in these muscles all the way. Let your head drop into a comfortable position and your jaw slacken as you concentrate on relaxing these muscles totally with your breathing exercise and mental command (trigger word). (You can also tense your neck muscles in other ways, such as bending your neck forward, backward, or to one side. Experiment to find the way that's best for you. Tense your jaw at the same time.)

7. Wrinkle your forehead and scalp upward to tense those muscles. Hold the tension for 5 seconds, then release it halfway for an additional 5 seconds. Then relax the tension away completely. Focus on relaxing your forehead and scalp muscles completely, and use your breathing and the associated mental command to deepen relaxation.

8. While sitting in a totally relaxed position, take a series of short inhalations, about 1 per second, until your chest is filled and tense. Hold this for about 5 seconds, then exhale slowly while thinking silently to yourself the word "relax" (or other trigger word). Most people can produce a deeply relaxed state by doing this. Repeat this exercise three times.

9. Finish off your relaxation practice by concentrating on breathing comfortably into your abdomen (rather than into your chest area). Simply let your stomach fill with air as you inhale and deepen your relaxing as you exhale. Abdominal breathing is far more relaxing than breathing into the chest.

Once you have mastered the nine-step approach described above, you can move to a more advanced level that involves combining muscle groups to provide a more general state of relaxation. Use the following three-step approach:

1. Tense all the muscles of the upper body simultaneously as you inhale. Hold for about 5 seconds, then release as you inhale and say your trigger word. Repeat the trigger word and deepen the relaxation as you exhale five more times.

2. Tense your entire lower body (hips, legs, and feet) as you inhale and hold for 5 seconds. Then, release the tension as you exhale and say your trigger word. Repeat the trigger word and deepen the relaxation as you exhale five more times.

3. Finally, tense all the muscles of your upper and lower body, hold for 5 seconds, then release the tension as you exhale and say the trigger word to yourself. Repeat the trigger word and deepen the relaxation as you exhale five more times.

Note that three things have been repeatedly associated with one another throughout your training: muscle relaxation, exhalation, and your trigger word. Thus, when you later use your trigger word and exhale, these actions should help to deepen your relaxation.

There are other steps you can take to make sure your relaxation skill transfers to the martial art studio. First, at home or at the studio, you can practice the relaxation response while holding a stance. Second, be sure to practice relaxation with exhalation and the trigger word while you are practicing on the floor. Practice your relaxation routine during your forms or while throwing some punches and incorporate it into your daily routine. The more you practice and apply the technique, the greater command you will have over this important skill.

Cognitive (mental) Relaxation

Cognitive relaxation clears the mind as well as relaxing the body. If you have had the experience of trying to go to sleep at night with a thousand thoughts going through your mind even though your body is relaxed, you know that you can be physically relaxed without being mentally relaxed.

The skill of cognitive relaxation can be mastered using a simple technique developed by Dr. Herbert Benson of Harvard University. Benson developed this easy-to-learn technique so that he could study the effects of meditation on the body. After studying a variety of Eastern and Western meditation practices, Benson concluded that four basic components are common to techniques such as yoga and transcendental meditation.

1. **A Quiet Environment**: Ideally, you should choose a quiet, calm environment with as few distractions as possible. The quiet environment contributes to the effectiveness of repeated word or phrase by making it easier to eliminate distracting thoughts.

2. **A Mental Device**: To shift the mind from logical thought, there should be a constant stimulus: a sound, a word, or a phrase repeated silently or aloud. Since one of the major difficulties in meditating is "mind wandering," the repetition of the word or phrase is a way to help break the train of distracting thoughts. Attention to the normal rhythm of breathing is also useful and helps direct attention inward.

3. **A Passive Attitude**: When distracting thoughts occur, they are simply to be ignored and attention redirected to the repetitive word and to the breathing. You should not worry about how well you are performing the technique, because this may well prevent the relaxation response from occurring. Adopt a "let it happen" attitude. The passive attitude is perhaps the most important element in eliciting the relaxation response. Distracting thoughts will occur. Do not worry about them. When these thoughts do present themselves and you become aware of them, simply return to the repetition of the mental device. These other thoughts do not mean you are performing the technique incorrectly. They are to be expected.

4. **A Comfortable Position**: A comfortable posture is important so that there is no undue muscular tension. Some methods call for a sitting position. A few practitioners use the cross-legged "lotus" position of the yogi. If you are lying down, there is a tendency to fall asleep (which means that this is a great

31

way to fall asleep if you are having difficulty doing so). The various postures of kneeling, swaying, or sitting in the cross-legged position are believed to have evolved to prevent falling asleep. You should be comfortable and relaxed.

Putting these elements together, here is how the Benson Meditation Technique is done:

1. Sit quietly in a comfortable position.
2. Close your eyes.
3. Deeply relax all your muscles, beginning at your feet and progressing up to your face. Keep them relaxed.
4. Breathe through your nose. Concentrate on your breathing. As you breathe out, say the word, "one" silently to yourself. For example, breathe in...out, "one"; In ...out, "one"; etc. Breathe easily and naturally.
5. Continue for 10 to 20 minutes. You may open your eyes to check the time, but do not use a loud alarm clock. When you finish, sit quietly for several minutes, at first with your eyes closed and later with your eyes open. Do not stand up for a few minutes.
6. Do not worry about whether you are successful in achieving a deep level of relaxation. Maintain a passive attitude and permit relaxation to occur at its own pace. When distracting thoughts occur, try to ignore them by not dwelling upon them and return to repeating "one.' With practice, the response should come with little effort. Practice the technique once or twice daily, but not within two hours after any meal, since the digestive processes seem to interfere with the elicitation of the relaxation response.

This meditation technique complements the progressive muscle relaxation technique used to teach somatic relaxation. Progressive relaxation is designed to help you learn a bodily response that you can apply quickly in performance situations to counteract emotional arousal or muscle tension. Obviously, you cannot sit down and meditate in the middle of competition. Meditation, on the other hand, produces mental as well as physical relaxation, and it can be used as a general stress reduction and energizing technique. Thus, both techniques are very useful, but in some what different ways.

7

Mental control of Emotions and stress

Martial Arts can be a very stressful occupation.
Practitioners must deal not only with the stresses of competition,
but also with the stresses of martial arts life away from the studio.
Separation from loved ones, difficulties with teachers or
classmates, dealing with uncertainty, and the seeming unfairness
that can so often occur in martial arts all add to the stresses
produced by slumps, poor performances, and other kinds of
adversity. Many practitioners fall by the wayside not because they
lack the coping skills to deal with the pressures on and off the
training floor. The ways in which practitioners think about and
react to the situations they encounter can influence their personal
happiness, their performance, and their ultimate success in martial
arts.

Thoughts and feelings are very closely connected to one
another. Our emotional reactions are almost always the result of
our general outlook or our interpretation of specific situations. We
are continually involved in talking to ourselves internally. Much of
this self-talk probably occurs beyond our conscious awareness. Our
habitual thinking patterns are carried out in a more or less
"automatic" fashion, like the well-practiced skills of driving an
automobile. However, people can learn to tune in to their self-talk
and become more aware of what they are telling themselves.

When we experience stress and other unpleasant emotions,
we usually view these reactions as being directly triggered by
disturbing situations. However, a careful analysis of what occurs
would disclose that when the upsetting event occurs, we tell
ourselves something about it ("This is awful!" They're screwing

things up for me!", etc.), and it is this self-statement that triggers the emotion. This sequence of events may be represented as:

Situation (A)—>Self-Statement (B)—>Emotion (C)
The A-B-C concept of emotion helps us understand why two different people can respond to the same situation with far different emotional reactions. It also suggests that by changing our internal self-statements at (B), we can change our emotional responses at (C). This can be accomplished by discovering what we are telling ourselves at (B), challenging those self-statements that are irrational and self-defeating, and replacing them with adaptive self-statements that decrease or prevent the emotional response.

This chapter will help you to learn and practice this important and effective means of coping with stress. Your task will be to learn to analyze specifically what you are saying internally to make yourself upset and to develop a set of specific self-statements that you can use to cope with disturbing situations. Thus, you will have a set of physical (relaxation) and mental (adaptive Self-statements) tools to cope with stress.

How We Distress Ourselves.
What kinds of self-statements are involved when we experience anxiety, anger, and other negative emotions? One way to find out is to stop whenever you find yourself getting upset and ask yourself what you are internally saying to yourself that is causing the distress. You will find that in most instances the sentences take forms such as, "Isn't it awful that...," or "Wouldn't it be terrible if...," or "What an (awful) (lousy) (rotten) thing for (me) (him) (her) (them) to do." In most cases you are either telling yourself that it is awful that things are not the way you demand that they be, or you are condemning yourself or someone else because your demands are not being met. (Often you will find that you are catastrophic about something over which you have no direct control.)

We use the term "catastrophe" to describe the kind of thinking that leads to much stress and emotional disturbance. By this we mean that relatively minor frustrations, inconveniences, and concerns are mentally blown up so that they become, for the moment, catastrophes which are emotionally reacted to as such (for it is appropriate to become very upset over true catastrophes). Much of our distress-producing thinking takes the form, "I don't like this situation! This is terrible! I can't stand it! It's driving me crazy! It shouldn't be this way! It's simply got to change or I can't possibly be happy!"

If you stop and ask yourself, "How is it terrible that...?" or "Why would it actually be awful if...?" or "Who am I to demand that things be exactly the way I'd like them to be?," you will often find that you quickly get over being upset because you can easily see the irrational aspects of what you are telling yourself. By systematically tuning in to your own internal statements about troublesome situations, you will find that you can pretty quickly pin down the thoughts that are producing your distress.

Stress-Reducing Thoughts.

A key to mentally coping with stress is awareness of the role that your own thoughts play in generating distress. Whenever you feel yourself becoming upset, the first thing you should tell yourself is: "I am creating this feeling by the way I'm thinking. How can I stop myself from being upset?" This statement, or one like it, will not only serve to place things in proper perspective by reminding you that your thinking, not the situation, is causing your feelings: but will also cause you to focus on your own stress-reducing thoughts. It immediately alerts you that it is time to use the physical relaxation and mental coping techniques that are essential stress management tools.

As noted above, we often catastrophe when things are not the way we want them to be and thereby create our own stress. In fact, we often change our desires into demands; preferences become musts, should, or sure necessities. Indeed, we can go even further and suggest that any time we experience unpleasant emotions (stress, anger, fear) it is because things for people (including ourselves) are not the way we want them to be. Thus, the idea that things should or must be the way we like them is an idea that we can focus on in developing stress-reducing thoughts. Here are some examples of self-statements that can be used to stop this irrational idea from triggering stress:

1. "I may not like this situation, but I certainly can live with it. No sense getting strung out."
2. "There's no reason why the world should revolve around my needs."
3. "Unfortunately, people don't always behave like I want them to. That's the way it goes--no use."
4. "Other people's needs are as important to them as mine are to me."
5. "I don't have to be perfect. I can make mistakes, too. I don't have to please everyone."
6. "O.K., so I don't like this. It's not the end of the world."
7. "Don't catastrophes, now. Put this in perspective."
8. "It would be nice if everything always went perfectly, but that's not the way life is."
9. "If I catastrophes about this, I deserve to be upset."
10. "If I can change this situation, I should do so. Thinking about what I can do about this situation is better than getting upset."
11. "It would be nice if life was fair, but it isn't always, especially in martial arts."
12. "Life is too short to let things like this make me miserable."

Here are some other examples of rational thinking that can help prevent a great deal of needless stress and emotional suffering:

1. All human beings, including instructors, coaches, classmates, school managers, and yourself, are fallible human beings who do the best they can but occasionally screw up. Demanding perfection from yourself or others is a losing proposition. Where you are concerned, strive to be the best that you can be, but don't demand perfection of yourself, or hinge your sense of self worth on being perfect. Perfection comes in the next life, not here. Winners strive for perfection; they don't demand it of themselves. That's why they can bounce back from adversity, knowing that they did everything in their control to do their best.

2. Your personal worth does not depend on your achievement. Many successful martial artists have received most of the recognition in their lives for their martial accomplishments, and it's easy for them to begin to define their self-worth in terms of their achievements. This is a losing proposition as well, because your worth as a person will be only as good as your last performance. Your martial arts skills are the frosting on the cake. Your true self-worth comes from the fact that you are an individual human being who is capable of good in many areas of life. Your basic worth as a human being will remain intact long after your martial arts career is over.

The flip side of this argument is that your skill as a martial artist does not make you an inherently more worthwhile human being than the receptionist, the vendor in the street, or the person who wants your autograph. They have the same inherent value you do, and they deserve to be treated with the same respect and dignity that you want for yourself. The world may tell you that you deserve more than others because of your talents, but it is important to realize that you did nothing to deserve the body and life circumstances that you were sent into this world with. Count your blessings, be grateful for them, and share the gifts you have been given with others. The final kick in your life won't be known for a long time.

3. As much as we would like it to be, life is not always fair. Demanding that it always treat you fairly is an exercise of frustration. There is much in life that is beyond your control, and some of those things may seem totally unfair to you. For example, you may feel that you have played well enough to be in the next competition or have been promoted to the next level. You may feel that you are not being given the opportunity you deserve. Yet, many factors influence the decisions that are made in martial arts, and bitterness over unfair treatment has ruined the path of many a practitioner.

On the other hand, there are many things over which you do have control, the major ones being your work habits, attitudes, effort, and ability to develop your skills. Focus on the things you

can control and work as hard as you can. Shut out the negative
thoughts and thereby short-circuit the negative emotions of anger,
depression, and anxiety that can undermine your effort and
performance. In martial arts, things can change very quickly, and
you owe it to yourself to be ready when opportunity knocks. And
remember, it may knock only once.

4. Finally, remember these key ideas:

*You feel the way you think.

*You can stand anything(unless you tell yourself you
can't).

*You, not situations, cause your emotions.

*You can always control your emotions with your
thinking.

These examples can help you to develop your own set of
self-statements for coping with difficult situations. You will find
that you can almost always short-circuit unpleasant emotions by
placing things in a non-catastrophizing perspective.

Analyzing Thoughts and Feelings

Mental control of emotions and stress requires that you
learn to substitute rational thoughts and beliefs for the self-
defeating and irrational thought patterns that cause disturbance.
Here is an exercise that will help you develop some new ways of
thinking about situations that cause you to generate distress for
yourself. Note that the steps are set up according to the A-B-C
theory of emotions that was discussed earlier. However, the steps
are set up in order that people usually think about stressful events:
A (the Activating event), C (the emotional consequence), and B (the
Belief or self-statement that caused C). Note, however, that a new
step, D (for Dispute) has been added. At this step, you dispute what
you must have told yourself about A in order to have become
disturbed, then substitute a new stress-reducing self-statement that
could have prevented the emotional reaction. This exercise is useful
in helping people develop a set of ideas that they can use in
upsetting situations.

Briefly answer the following questions about a recent event that you found disturbing:

A. What happened? Briefly describe the event.

C. How did you feel when(A) occurred? What was your emotional reaction to
(A)?

B. What must you have told yourself about (A) in order to produce (C)?
D. Instead of (B), what could you have told yourself about (A) that might have prevented (C)?

If you do this exercise repeatedly over a period of time, you will find that there are a relatively small number of irrational ideas that cause most of your disturbance. By analyzing and challenging those ideas and finding substitute self-statements, you will be developing powerful self-control weapons against stress. You will also find that at first, you will use the new statements to diffuse your emotions after you have begun to get upset. After awhile, however, your new ways of thinking will replace the old ones and will occur in response to the situations, thereby preventing you from becoming upset. You will then have acquired the same thought patterns as those people who are not easily upset.

Adaptive Self-Instructions
Intense emotions can often have a disruptive effect on performance. We can become so upset or angry that it is hard to function effectively. For example, some practitioners become so tense and anxious in pressure situations that they cannot perform well. One reason why intense emotions can disrupt performance is that people become so bound up in self-defeating thoughts about

how terrible the situation is or will be that they cannot devote full attention to what they should be doing in order to cope with the situation. These thoughts also create tension and increase arousal to a level that disrupts physical performance.

What is needed is a way to counteract the negative thinking and get attention back to the task at hand. Here are some self-instructions that practitioners have used to help them reduce stress and keep their minds on the task at hand:
1. "What is it that I have to do?"
2. "Don't think about being upset, just about what you have to do."
3. "Don't get all bent out of shape; just do what has to be done."
4. "Relax. You're in control. Take a deep breath."
5."This upset is a cue for you to use your coping skills. Relax and think rationally."
6. "Focus on the present. What is it you have to do?"

We all know that behaviors that lead to a positive outcome become stronger and more efficient. One important source of reward for saying adaptive things to yourself is that they work and help you control your level of stress. Used in conjunction with your relaxation coping response, they give you powerful weapons against negative emotions. You can help this strengthening process along by internally rewarding yourself immediately after you use them effectively. When you feel yourself handling stress effectively, reward yourself; you're winning out over your deadliest enemy. Here are some examples of rewarding self-statements:
1. "Way to go! You're in control."
2. "Good--you're handling the stress."
3. "Beautiful--you did it!"

Coping competently with life's stresses increases self-confidence and resiliency. By developing your coping abilities, you can gain increasing control over emotional life.

Mind-Body Control: The Integrated Coping Response

Stress is a mind-body process. In this chapter, we have talked about the mental part of stress. In the previous chapter on relaxation, we discussed the body's arousal reactions, which are also part of the stress response.

When you have developed both your relaxation skills and your set of stress-reducing self-statements, you can combine them into a powerful mind-body coping response that makes use of both sets of skills and works them into the breathing cycle so they can be used anywhere, at any time, without disrupting what you are doing. We call this the integrated coping response because it integrates the two sets of coping skills, relaxation and stress-reducing self-statements, into one highly effective coping response.

Recall that our somatic relaxation training program involved the repeated pairing of relaxation with (a) the exhalation or outbreath phase of the breathing cycle, and (b) a trigger word, such as "relax." Thus, to relax, you can say your trigger word as you exhale and let your muscles relax.

The integrated coping response simply involves adding in something during the inhalation phase of the breathing cycle: one of your stress-reducing or attention focusing self-statements. Thus, as you inhale, you say to yourself the appropriate self-statement. As you pause at the top of the breathing cycle, you can say a connecting word like "so" or "and." Then, as you slowly exhale, say your trigger word and let your muscles relax completely. The sequence, with some examples included, is shown in Figure below.

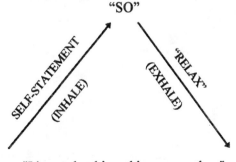

"It's not that big a thing...so...relax."
"I may not like this, but I can definitely stand it...so...relax."
"I need to concentrate, not to make myself uptight...so...relax."
"I'm in control...so...relax."

MENTAL SKILLS

The integrated coping response can be done repeatedly, with each breath cycle for a time if, desired. You can change the self-statement as often as you wish until you find the one that is most effective in the particular situation you are dealing with. It can also be worked into your performance routine, with the self-statement being a self-instruction. Examples might be, "see the punch...and...relax" as a kicker readies himself in the arena, or "Inside punch...and...loose" as a puncher readies himself before the fight.

Stress can take many forms, and it can become the martial artist's worst enemy if it is not mastered. The relaxation and mental-control skill that go into the integrated coping response are proven performance-enhancers, but their usefulness extends far beyond martial arts. They have been learned by people in countless walks of life to gain control over their emotional lives and to live more enjoyably. You certainly owe it to yourself to expand the effort and dedication required to learn these skills well, for they will benefit you not only in martial arts, but in other areas of your life as well.

8

IMAGERY: USING THE MIND TO PROGRAM THE BODY

"Right before a fight, I lie down, close my eyes, relax my body, and prepare myself for the fight. I go through the entire makeup of the other fighter, one punch at a time. I visualize exactly how I am going to punch him, and I see and feel myself throwing exactly the punches that I what to throw.
Before I ever begin to warm up in the dressing room, I've faced all of my opponents punches four times and I've gotten my body ready for exactly what it is I want to do."

The speaker was Juan Laporte, one of the great lightweights of his time. In 1992, when he was coaching some youngsters in Gleason's Gym, I asked Juan to talk about the mental side of his boxing. He told me that the mental skills he had developed over the years were every bit as important to his success as his physical talent. Among those skills is the ability to relax and maintain his concentration under even the most adverse conditions and the ability to program himself through mental rehearsal.

Juan Laporte is only one of many great fighters who have incorporated mental rehearsal, or imagery, into their boxing plan. Here is how Merqui Sosa described his use of imagery:

"The night before a fight, I visualize the opponent and the punches I'm going to see the next day. I hit the opponent right on the button and know what it is going to feel like. I hit the punches where I want to. I keep some gloves at home. If I want a stronger

picture, I put them on and do some shadow boxing in the living room."

David Brown, a young boxer I met at Gleasons, carried his imagery routine into the ring itself and incorporated it into each round. I start toward the middle of the ring, and I imagine myself hitting the "Sweet Spot" in the body area just as the opponent is moving in. I see a line and the punch going through. It's important for me to see myself punching there and not swinging at him. I remind myself to see the release and the twist behind the punch, then I "see it" the way I'm going to see it.

It goes by a variety of names: " visualization," "mental rehearsal," "or Imagery." I prefer the terms mental rehearsal or imagery rather than visualization because, as we have seen in the foregoing examples, mental rehearsal involves far more than simply "seeing with the mind's eye." Effective mental rehearsal involves all of the senses, including feeling the activity of one's muscles as they perform the skill. Whatever term you prefer, however, there is no question that mental rehearsal is one of the most powerful techniques for programming the body to perform as you want it to.

People in all walks of life, including many great martial artists, have used imagery to enhance their performance. Moreover, research has supported the claims of many martial artists that imagery improves their performance. Recent surveys of the scientific literature have concluded that although physical practice is the most effective way to learn a skill, mental practice can sometimes be as effective as physical practice in improving performance.

All of us have had firsthand experience in ways that our imagination can affect our thoughts, feelings, and behavior. Can you recall instances in which you experienced excitement by thinking about the gift you might receive for your birthday or Christmas, or by imagining a reunion with your spouse or girlfriend? Can you recall an instance in which you experienced the "dreads" by anticipating something very bad that might happen to you? When you were a child first beginning to practice martial arts, can you remember imitating the stances, punching form, or kicking techniques of your martial arts heroes? In all of these instances, imagery was involved. To imitate your martial arts hero, you had to be able to imagine his stance, how he punched, how he would move and throw the kick, or how he evaded a strike before you could copy it. Perhaps you even put yourself in his place, performing the same actions in a major competition situated in your mind.

Imagery training involves the systematic use of mental rehearsal to program yourself for improved performance. It can be used as a means of learning or perfecting a skill level while recovering from an injury, or developing a "fight plan". Before discussing these uses of mental rehearsal, let us consider the nature of imagery and the principles that account for its effectiveness.

Understanding Imagery

Imagery involves using any or all the senses to create or recreate an experience in the mind. Although imagery is often termed visualization, sight is not the only sense that can be used. Imagery can involve not only sights, but sounds, tastes, smells, sensations of the body movements, or touch sensations. The more senses we can involve in our images, the more vivid the images are likely to be. Thus, a pugilist can image the sight of a kick , the feel of heaviness in his punches, the body sensation as he strides around his opponent, the crack of the punch at making contract, and the feeling in the hands as they go through the opponent.

Imagery can be used not only to recreate experiences we have had in the past, but also to create new ones. Although imagery is based on our memories, the brain is able to put elements of memory together to create new experiences. For example, boxer Ray Leonard used imagery to create offensive plans against defenses he had not yet faced. After viewing films of the opponent's defense, he used imagery to create successful offensive patterns against that defense. In the same way, a martial artist can watch a sparring partner on video and create images of exactly how he would like to fight that person.

How does imagery work? How can simply imagining an action lead to an actual improvement in performance? The answer is that when we learn or perfect a skill, tiny "electrical circuits" are established in the nervous system and in the muscles that perform the act. Thus, when the martial artist engages in martial movements, the brain is constantly transmitting impulses to the muscles for the production of the movements. The reason imagery works is that similar impulses occur in the brain and muscles when the martial artist imagines the movements without actually performing them. Electrical recordings from the brain and muscles suggest that low-level firing of nerve and muscle cells creates, in the nervous system and muscles, a kind of blueprint to help the individual execute the movement later on. According to Dr. Maxwell Maltz, this is sometimes called "muscle memory."

In one interesting demonstration, an Olympic downhill skier was asked to recreate a race by using imagery. The electrical activity in the skier's leg muscles was monitored and recorded by a polygraph as he imagined the downhill run over the familiar course. The printout of the muscle firings mirrored the terrain of the ski run. His muscle firings increased in speed and intensity at certain points during imagery that corresponded to difficult turns and rough sections on the run.

Whether the martial artist actually performs movements or vividly imagine performing them, performance circuits in the brain and muscles are activated and strengthened. This means that the martial artist may actually strengthen the nervous pathways for certain movements in his style. Indeed, research in the former Soviet Union and in many of our universities here in the States has shown that a mixture of mental rehearsal and physical practice actually results in a higher level of subsequent performance on athletic tasks than does 100% physical practice.

If mental rehearsal is so effective, why doesn't every martial artist make use of it? My experience has been that many martial artists who would like to use imagery feel that their imaginations are not strong enough to create vivid images. However, research has shown that it is not necessary to create "photographic" images. Actually, few people can do that, although imagery, like any other skill, improves with practice. All that is really necessary is to have a general "feel" for what you want to do in the beginning. With time and practice, the images will become more and more vivid. The most effective visualization will result for those who try to create specific and detailed images that involve all of the appropriate senses: vision, hearing, touch, and sensations of the body movement. As a martial artist, you surely have enough specific experience to create the images you need. You know what you want your body to do.

Here is a little demonstration that will show you the power of imagination to influence the actions of the body. Attach an object such as a ring to a string approximately twelve inches long. Resting your elbow on the table top, lightly hold one end of the string between your thumb and forefinger with the weight suspended directly below. Now, focusing carefully on the weight, imagine in your mind's eye the weight moving right and left like the pendulum of a clock. Continue to imagine that as vividly as you can. You will probably find that after awhile, with no voluntary effort on your part, the weight actually begins to move back and forth. When that happens, change the image so that the weight swings directly away from and then toward the chest. Once that occurs, try images of the weight moving in a clockwise circle and then finally, in a counter-clockwise circle. In doing this exercise, you will be amazed at how just imagining the movement soon produced the actual movement.

Experiencing Imagery

As you do these exercises, remember that imagery is more than just seeing or visualizing something in your mind's eye. Vivid images may involve not only visualizing, but any of the senses. Along with these sensations, you may also experience emotions, moods, or certain states of mind. As you imagine the general situations described below, try to provide as much detail from your imagination as possible to make the images just as real as you can.

Afterwards, you will be asked to note how vividly you saw or visualized the situation, how clearly you heard the sounds, how vividly you felt your body movements (kinesthetic sense) during the activity, and how clearly you were aware of your state of mind or felt the emotions of the situation.

After you read each general description, think of a specific example of it: the time, the place, the people involved, the skill. Next, close your eyes and use breathing and relaxation skills to become as relaxed as you can. Imagery becomes more vivid when we are relaxed. Put aside all other thoughts for the moment, keep your eyes as vivid as you can. Remember, there are no right or wrong images. Use your imagery skills to develop as vivid and clear an image as possible.

After you have completed the imagery, rate the images you produced by circling the number that best describes the image you had.

> 1=No image present
> 2=Not clear or vivid, but could be recognized
> 3=Moderately clear and vivid image
> 4=Clear and vivid image
> 5=Extremely clear and vivid image; almost like being there

Exercise-1: Practicing a skill

Select one specific skill that you want to work on in practice. It may be throwing a punch, kicking practice, or playing forms. Now imagine yourself performing this activity at the place where you would normally practice it. See and feel yourself performing just the way you want to. Do it again and again. Keep your attention directed on this activity as you would want to during the real practice. See and feel yourself performing just the way you want to. See it from the inside, again and again. See the punch; hear the crack of the kick or feel the torque of the body when playing the forms; feel the fluid motion of your muscles as you perform the skill; experience the mood or emotions that you feel, or the state of mind you are experiencing.

Close your eyes now and simply relax and run the movie in the theater of your mind for about a minute.

When you have completed the imagery, answer the following question:

1.Rate how vividly you saw or visualized the image:

1 2 3 4 5

2.Rate how well you heard the sounds during the imagery:

1 2 3 4 5

3.Rate how vividly you felt your body movements during the activity:

1 2 3 4 5

4.Rate how clearly you were aware of your mood:

1 2 3 4 5

Exercise 2. Performing in sparring.

Consider now a weakness in your fighting, a skill that you need to improve. Place yourself in a sparring situation and vividly imagine yourself making exactly the adjustment you need to make in order to perform this skill correctly. For example, if you have been punching with the elbow out, imagine yourself (from the inside) keeping your elbow tucked-in and executing a perfect punch. Feel your body reacting just as you want it to. See the punch. Hear the crack of the punch when making contact. If you're a kicker, vividly see the opponent give you the target. Feel yourself move into position with a beautiful, fluid motion and see the kick going to its target with exactly the movement you want. Hear the kick pound into the opponents body. Whatever the skill, visualize it from the inside as vividly as you can. Relax, close your eyes, and rehearse the scene again and again for a minute.

When you finish, rate the quality of your imagery in the same manner as before.

1. Rate how vividly you saw or visualized the image:

1 2 3 4 5

2. Rate how well you heard the sounds during the imagery:

1 2 3 4 5

3. Rate how vividly you felt your body movements during the activity:

1 2 3 4 5

4. Rate how clearly you were aware of your mood:

1 2 3 4 5

Using Imagery Effectively

One of the benefits of relaxation training is that it can make your visualization more vivid and effective. Research has shown that a combination of relaxation and visualization produces better performance results than imagery alone. Moreover, the relation between imagery and relaxation is a two-way street; we can also use imagery to enhance relaxation. One technique that many martial artists have used is to create in your mind the most relaxing setting that you can think of. It may be, for example, a special place, such as a warm tropical beach where you can relax totally. If you think of such a place and visualize it repeatedly, you will find that you can quickly return to your "relaxing place" to produce a state of relaxation. One prominent martial artist told me that when he begins to get tense, he can immediately create a state of relaxation by imagining himself in a warm, soothing whirlpool bath. Another reported that when he has trouble going to sleep because of intrusive thoughts or images, he creates a blank movie screen in his mind. Each time he inhales, he imagines the breath sucking all thoughts out of his mind to create a blank, relaxed state. As he exhales, he imagines sinking deeper into a warm relaxing void and uses the trigger word "slee-ee-p". These imagines usually allow him to fall asleep almost immediately.

Imagery is a very personal thing. You will find through experimentation that you can develop many ways to use imagery to create relaxation, on the one hand, or to get yourself energized, on the other.

Imagery and Concentration

Imagery and concentration also are a two-way street. On the one hand, imagery requires that you be able to concentrate on the images and control them to some extent. This skill develops as you use imagery repeatedly. In turn, imagery can be used to increase concentration. For example, a practitioner working on his distance awareness can repeatedly imagine seeing a kick come out of the opponent's chamber at the release point and follow it all the way to interception. He can imagine recognizing different kicks by picking up the spin on the kick or the way it is released by the kicker. This exercise can help improve his concentration and his ability to more consistently "see the kick" in sparring situations. Likewise, kickers can use imagery to improve their concentration on the receiver's target. They can learn to block out the counter-attacker altogether, as one of my contemporaries was able to do. During his later years of training, he told me that when he played sticking hands (an exercise in the Ving Tsun Kung Fu system), he ignored the opponent and simply played developing his own attributes. He attributed a visualization routine involving "lines" to the target that he developed and perfected for his tremendous powers of concentration.

Imagery can also help a practitioner restore concentration when he loses it. If you are distracted during a sparring session, you can step out of the ring or the training floor, take a deep breath and relax, and gently bring your attention back by mentally rehearsing the next punch that you are going to see or throw.

Practicing Martial Skills

We have already discussed the use of imagery in practicing martial arts skills. It is again well to emphasize that this is one of the most important uses of imagery.

Many practitioners use imagery in conjunction with watching a tape of themselves. For example, a kicker may see a tape of himself when he was really going well, and use that as a basis for imagery. Likewise, a puncher may view a tape showing a defect in his delivery and use this information as a way of making the proper adjustment, first in imagery, and then on the mound.

We can learn a great deal from observing other practitioners. One effective way of using such observation is to watch a practitioner who performs a skill exactly as you would like to perform it. Then use that information to create images of yourself performing in exactly that way. Many practitioners who have used this technique have been delighted with the results when they begin performing the skill exactly as the practitioner who served as the model does.

Preparing to Perform

Imagery has been used by many pugilists as a way of preparing themselves for sparring situations. Earlier, we saw how Juan Laporte began his preparation the night before he boxed by going through the entire round and imagining himself throwing exactly the punches that he wanted to throw his opponent. However, when Laporte was going to fight against the great Julio Caesar Chavez, he was probably unaware that at another location in town, Chavez was doing exactly the same preparation: "The night before the fight I think about every punch he might throw me, and then, after I've seen that punch once the next day, my picture of that punch is so strong, if he made any kind of mistake, I would do some damage."

As noted earlier, one of my contemporaries prepared himself for his session of sticking hands by visualizing lines. A boxing legend, Joe Louis routine was described as follows: The night of the fight, he'll come in after a short warm-up, lie down on the training table, and close his eyes. A lot of people think he's sleeping. But what he's thinking about are lines in the target. He thinks about outer gates and inner gates. He doesn't ever think about anything over the target. And by not thinking about it, he gets himself working that way.

Mental preparation can occur not only before a fight, but literally, from punch to punch. For example, when I throw a bad punch at a bad target or fail to land a kick on a good target, I immediately step out of the critical zone and used imagery to make an adjustment. "I think about what I didn't like and fix it in my mind. I don't analyze it. I see, feel, and hear myself getting the results I want."

As you will see later when we discuss punching and kicking routines, imagery should always be part of those success chains. Before every punch, a practitioner can use imagery to program himself to throw the punch he wants. Likewise, a kicker can use imagery to maintain relaxation, to prepare himself to see the target well, and to imagine himself reacting appropriately to the sparring situation. For example, with an opponent who drops his right hand, a puncher should imagine himself hitting the target to the right side to advance the attack. Doing so helps keep him focused on his task and also programs his body to do what he wants it to do.

Using Triggers to Increase Imagery Effectiveness

Triggers are words or phrases that help you focus on the correct cues or actions during imagery. Triggers help to program the proper image, and the trigger words can also be used when actually performing the action. An example might be "see the opening," which was used by counter punching great Wilfredo Benitez to focus his attention on the opponents release point. Another fighter used "zoom" (as in zoom lens) to concentrate all his attention on the release point. "Down the line" might be used by a hitter who wants to emphasize that mechanic. One of my students used "Whip" to help create the image of a fluid, yet explosive release of the punch; another used "on top" to reinforce the image of how he wanted to throw his kick. Still another said "chest" to keep his attention focused on the opponent's target.

To develop your trigger words, analyze exactly what your performance objective is, then try to find a key word or phrase that captures what you are trying to do. Make the words as vivid as possible. By incorporating the trigger word into your imagery, you will increase its vividness and reinforce the action during imagery and will become part of the mind-muscle program that performs the act. This means that you can use the trigger when you are actually performing and it will help program the behavior. Sometimes during my early training years I was able to use as a trigger word, "Easy...just let it flow." This helped keep me loose and focused.

Rehearsing Sparring Situations

Sparring can easily be won or lost on the basis of how practitioners react to fighting situations. A punch to the wrong target, missing the kick, or failing to follow up on an attack can be very costly. "Being in the fight" means knowing the combative situation and preparing yourself to make the correct move if a particular situation arises.

Imagery can be an important part of making the right move. Many teachers and coaches have stressed the importance of imagining beforehand what you will do with the technique if the attack is entering your boundary or which counter-attack you will use on the opponent for that particular move. An infighter must know where the opponent is going to be and cut him off understanding the fighting situation. Imagery can be used to program yourself to react automatically to the particular fighting situation.

Fighting Slumps with Imagery

The skills in martial arts are so delicate and complex that it is very easy to fall into a mechanical rut and see performance begin to decline. The result can be a dreaded slump which is both psychological and physical in nature.

Imagery can help with both the mechanical and the psychological aspects of the slump. By using his imagination, a practitioner can take mental practice in the arena, on the training floor, or in the streets. By comparing tapes of previous good performances with current performances, a practitioner may detect the mechanical flaw and then use imagery to help himself get back to the techniques that were successful for him. He can "rerun" his performances, seeing the punches and moves that were unsatisfactory and then making the adjustments.

Visualization also is useful from a psychological perspective, for the essence of a slump is a sense of frustration that one has somehow "lost it." By replaying the past successes and making adjustments in the theater of the mind, visualization can keep a practitioner positive and reduce the feelings of helplessness that often accompany a slump.

Imagery and Injuries

When practitioners are injured, they must cope with pain, inactivity, and inability to practice their skills physically. Research, as well as reports of many martial artists, indicate that imagery can serve useful functions during the recovery period.

Golfer Jack Nicklaus is a leading proponent of imagery. He states that he uses imagery before every shot that he takes. On one occasion, he reported that he had been having a great deal of difficulty with chip shots. To make matters worse, he had suffered an injury that made it impossible for him to practice for several weeks. During the healing period, he mentally practiced hundreds of chip shots a day and was delighted to find that when he returned to action, his ability to make chip shots had greatly improved.

A martial artist can use imagery in the same fashion while recovering from injury. A puncher can take hundreds of swings a day in his mental arena, and a kicker can throw hundreds of kicks daily from his mental sparring space. Such practice can help eliminate some of the rustiness caused by physical inactivity.

Research has shown that imagery can be used in a variety of ways to deal with pain. First, it can be used as a distraction from the pain sensations. Vividly imagining a relaxing or pleasurable scene can help counteract the sensations of pain. Imagery can also be used to modify the pain sensation themselves. You can focus your attention on the pain itself, and imagine it softening, spreading out and slowly dissolving. You can also give the pain a color, such as hot red and then imagine the pain becoming a soft, soothing blue.

Studies of people who have a strong ability to tolerate pain indicate that they frequently use imagery in these ways.

Finally, medical research has shown that imagery can actually speed the physical healing process. We know that the physiology of the body can be very strongly affected by imagery, but the key is to know what to imagine. If you have an injury, talk to someone in the medical sports field and find out as much as you can about (a) the nature of the injury, and (b) exactly what will happen to the injured part as it heals. Have the medical expert draw you a picture of the injured part, if necessary, and ask him what it would look like if you could somehow do time lapse photography inside the body to record the healing process. For example, he might tell you that as a pulled hamstring heals, the swelling produced by fluid from the damaged muscle tissue will dissipate and the blood supply to the injured muscle will gradually restore its looseness and flexibility. You can use this information to then imagine the process of healing again and again. In this way, you can use your mind to help your body heal.

Some Final Thoughts

Mental rehearsal is most effective when it is carried out in a systematic manner. To be systematic, daily imagery practice is advised. As Bruce Lee, Ali, and other greats have done, you can easily get into the habit of making imagery a part of your daily routine. Simply set aside ten minutes in a quiet place under relaxing conditions to do your daily imagery. Work on the skills you want to improve as well as the ones you are performing well.

Imagery can be done before physical practice sessions, and doing so may help you get more out of the practice itself. It may also be done after actual physical practice sessions to reinforce what you did well and help you make adjustments. Imagery can be used as part of a performance routine, such as before each sparring session, and it can be used during the fight before actually performing a skill. Finally, a good time to use imagery is after competition. Using imagery at this time helps you to reinforce what you did well and helps you make the necessary adjustments to improve performance.

There are many ways in which the mind can interfere with performance. On the other hand, mental rehearsal is a proven tool that can help you take your performance to higher levels.

9

CONCENTRATION

One of the most critical of all performance skills is the ability to concentrate. Concentration is the ability to focus one's attention on the task at hand while being unaffected by irrelevant external or internal stimuli. External stimuli may include a booing crowd, sideline comments, a heckling fan, or bad referee calls. Internal distracters include body sensations of fatigue or pain, emotional responses such as anxiety or anger, or thoughts such as "I gotta hit him," "Don't let this guy hit me," or "I blew it!" Thus, concentration is a learned skill of not reacting to or being distracted by irrelevant stimuli. It involves being totally in the here and now, in the present. When our minds are focused on the past or on the future, we cannot be as effective in our present performance.

The ability to concentrate is a skill, and like any other skill, it can be developed and improved through practice. We can learn to decrease attention to irrelevant stimuli and to increase attention to the task at hand when we lose concentration.

In developing your concentration, knowing what to focus on is as critical as knowing how to control your focus of attention. A practitioner may have excellent concentration skills, but if he is focusing on the wrong things, the skills will not be very helpful. For example, when Ping arrived at the Ving Tsun Kung Fu Studio, his reactions to oncoming attacks were considered below par. With a great deal of hard work and practice, his reactions improved tremendously. He attributed his quick reactions to change in his focus of attention. Instead of simply watching the opponent, Ping said, he learned to focus his attention totally on the zone of the person in front of him where the puncher's hand would have to

58

make contact with *his* own. He practiced this focus of attention every day during sticking hand practice as well as in his sparring. With his new focus of attention, which became "automatic" through practice and repetition, Ping was able to immediately parry and react to a barrage of punches and kicks.

Sometimes, the appropriate focus of attention is internal rather than external. For example, many veteran martial artists are able to become aware of feedback from their muscles as they punch or kick. With this skill, they can quickly detect any flaw in their delivery and make the appropriate adjustment. Veteran fighters learn to do the same thing, hereby becoming their own coaches.

Concentration involves not only focusing on what is relevant, but also being able to ignore or block out the irrelevant. The most damaging internal distracters are negative thoughts that deflect attention away from the task at hand. One of the reasons why most martial artists report that it is much easier to concentrate when they are performing well is that these negative thoughts are unlikely to occur. When things are going poorly, however, it can be very hard to keep one's mind clear and focused. Experienced martial artists have found that the best way to turn off negative and interfering thoughts is not by trying to suppress them, but by being able to concentrate so strongly on the task at hand that the thoughts simply fade away into the background. Thus, as in all the skills I emphasize, the positive approach to increasing what one wants to do is better than trying to eliminate what one does not want to.

Controlling the Focus of Attention

For people who have good concentration skills, the focus of attention can operate a bit like zoom lens on a camera. The lens can retract to provide a wide angle view, as might be needed by a puncher who is scanning the opponent to see how the defense is positioned against him. When necessary, however, the lens can also zoom in on a very small portion of the scene, as when a kicker focuses totally on the opponent's head.

To appreciate the difference between broad, or soft focus, and narrow, or hard focus, pick out some object across the room directly in front of you. While looking directly ahead and not moving your eyes, try to see as much of the room and the objects in the room as your peripheral vision will allow. You are now in broad, or soft focus.

Picture now a broad funnel into which your mind is moving. Centered in the middle of the funnel is the object directly across the room from you. Gradually narrow your focus by narrowing the funnel so the only thing in your focus of attention is the object across from you. When your attention is focused totally on that object, you are in narrow focus, widening the funnel until you can again see everything in the room. Then, repeat the process of zooming in on the object in front of you.

The Soft Focus-Hard Focus Routine

The soft focus-hard focus sequence is a very important skill. Soft focus is much easier to do than the hard, or narrow focus. In fact, most people can only hold the hard focus for a few seconds at a time without becoming quite fatigued. Because so many important acts of concentration in martial arts, such as seeing the punch as it is released by the opponent, focusing totally on the opponent's body, and picking up on the kick before it reaches its target, or hard focus, martial artists need to develop an attention pattern that allows them to zoom in on the relevant stimulus at just the right moment. One very effective stimulus at just the right moment. One very effective method of doing so is the soft focus-hard focus routine.

This routine involves maintaining a relaxed soft focus until the specific point at which you need to lock in on the target, then shifting rapidly to the needed hard focus. The timing of this shift is very important, and it must be practiced in order to be perfected. Thus, Michael shifts to a hard focus on the contact zone in front of the opponent as the rival begins toward him. The important thing about the shift is the contrast in detail that allows you to vividly concentrate on the attack or the opponent when you shift to hard focus. Michael said that he was able to completely tune out everything around the sparring area except the lines to the opponent target. Likewise, Michael stated that his focus on the opponent's release point is at times so good that he can literally see the attack coming off the opponents chamber position and pick up the kick immediately. Obviously, this level of concentration has required a great deal of practice on the part of both of these martial artists.

Next time you are on the training floor, experiment with the soft focus-hard focus shift. If you are next to spar, you might wish to begin by standing on the side of the sparring area (which, by the way, is a good place to practice your concentration skill of seeing the punches and kicks). Focus your attention quite broadly on the attacker's body and the surrounding area, perhaps even having the opponent be slightly out of focus. Then, at the point in his delivery where the attacker's hands part, zoom in on the release point while saying to yourself, "See the opening".

If you are a puncher, the time you are shadowboxing on the side or in the ring, try a similar soft focus-hard focus shift with your sparring partner. You will need to experiment to find the point at which it is best for you to zoom into hard focus on the opponent's target.

Practicing Your Concentration Skills

Like the other skills that we have discussed, concentration is not likely to develop to its maximum if it is practiced only under sparring conditions. As we have already seen, practice situations provide many opportunities to work on concentration abilities. For example, while loosening up before sparring, a practitioner can be working on refining his attention skills by throwing every punch to a specific target (for example, one to his partner's left shoulder, next to the right shoulder, one to the stomach, and a kick to each knee). Thus, the simple session of warming up becomes an opportunity to practice a soft focus-hard focus shift and to increase one's punching accuracy.

For those willing to pay the price of hard work and total effort, striking powers of concentration can be developed.

61

Mental rehearsal can also be an effective way of working on concentration skills. A practitioner can close his eyes and practice his attention skills through mental rehearsal. For example, a puncher or a kicker can practice the soft focus-hard focus shift through visualization.

Several of the skills that we have already discussed can be great aids to maintaining concentration. First of all, we are able to concentrate much better when we are relaxed. Therefore, the relaxation skills discussed earlier in the book can be very useful aids to maintaining concentration, particularly under stressful conditions. Likewise, the methods that we use for attacking and modifying self-defeating thought patterns can help a practitioner to gain control over distracting self-statements that can increase anxiety and deflect attention away from the task at hand. Finally, as we have just seen, imagery can be used to help a martial artist maintain concentration.

Recovering From Distractions

When attention is disrupted by either internal or external distracters, a practitioner may experience a "blooming, buzzing confusion" that makes concentration almost impossible. When this happens, a practitioner needs a way to gather his attention and recoups on the task at hand.

Several strategies have proven effective in this regard.

One method of recovering concentration is to focus completely on one's breathing (a skill that will be greatly enhanced through relaxation training). By shifting focus to a specific source of stimulation (in this case, his breathing), a martial artist can block out the distracting stimuli.

Another strategy is to select a specific external stimulus to focus on. For example, a kicker may choose a specific target on his sparring partner that is complicated and interesting. When needing to regain his concentration, the kicker might step off the sparring area, turn toward the opponent and focus his attention completely on that target, picking out every detail. This is, of course, simply a device for directing and focusing his attention. When his attention is totally focused and the previous "shotgunning" of attention has been overcome, the kicker can refocus his attention back to his task.

Finally, imagery can be used to regain concentration. Thus, as soon as a practitioner realizes that he is losing his concentration, he can stop himself, take a deep breath to relax and then bring his attention back by mentally rehearsing what he should be doing next.

The principle underlying all three of these strategies is this: When attention is disrupted, find a way to focus on a specific internal or external stimulus, thereby regaining control over your attention focus. Then shift your focus back to the task at hand.

One of the most powerful means of consistently attaining a high level of concentration is the performance routine. The end point of the performance routine should be focused concentration on the task at hand. Let us, therefore, consider the nature and the purpose of the performance routines or rituals that great performers use to get themselves into the ideal performance state and remain there.

10

PERFORMANCE ROUTINES: PUTTING IT ALL TOGETHER

Most good performers have routines or rituals that they use to prepare themselves for top performance. You've observed them in punchers and kickers in kung fu, karate, judo, and boxing. Over time, the performance routine can become a powerful trigger for creating the ideal performance state. The routine can help in deepening concentration, staying loose and relaxed, raising intensity, and turning on the automatic. The most valuable performance routines incorporate the psychological skills that we have already discussed in a manner that is uniquely suited for each martial artist. Thus, a routine should be put together very carefully and incorporate the elements that help you to consistently attain an optimal performance state.

A performance routine can be likened to a chain. Each link of the chain is a behavior on your part that has a definite purpose in leading you to your optimal state. When a consistent routine is performed repeatedly, each link in the chain becomes a trigger for the next link, and the final link in the chain is exactly the state that you want to be in. Done correctly, your performance routine is a very powerful method for gaining consistency in both your mental and physical state, and in performance. Moreover, the performance routine can be a very effective means of avoiding distraction and remaining focused on what you need to do at the moment.

Many great martial artists have a step-by-step routine that they use to get ready to perform.

The Fighters Success Chain

The performance routine suggested for fighters begins long before the competition and continues into the arena.

The Night Before, or Day of, the Competition

Your planning should begin long before the competition. Using imagery, you should mentally rehearse facing the opponents you are likely to see in the arena. Form vivid images of the way their punches behave, and the way you will hit the target. Virtually all of the great fighters report that they use mental rehearsal as part of their pre-fight preparation. You may also wish to incorporate the relaxation or meditation techniques learned in the stress management section to relax and energize yourself.

Before the Fight

Watch the opposing opponent warm up, focus on his speed and punches. Note whether he seems to be having any difficulty in controlling one of his techniques. If, for example, he seems to be having trouble with his side kick, you may expect to see more round house as he goes to his strength.

In the Waiting Area

Study the fighter, noting what he is throwing and what you can handle. Talk to teammates about techniques and visualize how he's fought you in the past and what you're likely to see. Develop your plan, taking into account tournament circumstances. Visualize past successes and your own strengths--- how you match best and how you can get your technique, and not his.

In the Corner

Get relaxed, and take practice punches with any necessary self-reminders about mechanics. This is the only time you should think about mechanics unless you need to adjust after a technique. Time the opponent's delivery as you take your practice swings.

Visualize what you will see, and see/feel/hear yourself hitting your opponent hard. Mentally rehearse parrying punches or kicks. Allow only positive thoughts and images: what you want to do, not what you don't want to do. Program yourself for success.

Outside the Arena

Relax yourself with breathing and your trigger word for relaxation. Combine your trigger word with the exhalation or outbreath. Breathe into your stomach, not into your chest. Clear your mind by focusing on your breathing.

Inside the Arena

Step into the ring and do a set of pre-punching/kicking routine that is compatible with relaxation and a relaxed rhythm. For example, you might punch/kick in a loose, relaxed manner. Do not vary this routine. If anything disrupts it, step aside and start over. Remember, the arena is your domain as a fighter. Take charge of it and yourself.

Concentrate only on seeing the punches. Use soft focus-hard focus to the release point. Your mind should be clear and focused on the only thing that matters: seeing this punch/kick from the release point into your zone. Let yourself be on automatic pilot, so that your reflexes operate freely and take your hands to the target.

Notice that this recommended routine incorporates all of the skills discussed so far. It involves goal setting and planning, relaxation, imagery, self-instructions, and concentration. By incorporating these skills into your routine, they will occur automatically as your routine becomes well-learned and automatic.

After Each Technique

Let go completely of the last technique. Its only importance is the feedback it gives you for completing the next technique. Make a mental adjustment through visualization if necessary. All that matters is the next technique.

Practicing Your Performance Routine

Remember, the goal of a performance routine is to get yourself on "automatic pilot" both mentally and physically. In order for this to occur, you must practice your performance routine so that it becomes so ingrained that almost nothing can disrupt it. To accomplish this goal, you cannot simply practice your performance routine in competition situations; you must also apply it in practice situations and in imagery.

Your practice will become even more productive if you incorporate your performance routine into them. Thus, when sparring, when you're throwing punches/kicks, or when you're playing forms make sure that you use your performance routine. Be like Bruce Lee, who made every technique in practice the same as a punch or kick thrown at him in sparring. As a fighter, for example, carry your performance routine into the ring as you warm up, when you're doing balance drills, or when you're throwing punches/kicks in the corner of the ring. The more you practice these skills and get them ingrained, the more automatic they will be and more consistently you will be able to overcome distractions and adversity, and perform as you wish.

You can also practice your performance routine in imagery and it is recommended that you do so. When you are doing mental rehearsal, take yourself through the entire routine a number of times. As you can see, developing and perfecting a performance routine takes some work on your part. A lazy martial artist will not do it; he will trust things to "take care of themselves." A dedicated martial artist, on the other hand, will see the performance routine for what it is: a means of performing more consistently in his optimal state. A winner will realize that his career is squarely in his own hands and will do whatever it takes to perfect both his mental and physical skills.

A Final Word

The skills described in this book will not be perfected simply by reading about them. They take work and effort on your part. If you wish to be the best martial artist you can be, you must perfect the mental side of your art as well as the physical. Goals without a determination to achieve them are useless. As a martial artist, you have to decide what price you are willing to pay to become the best that you are capable of becoming. A martial artist's responsibility for his career begins with a willingness to acknowledge who he is and what he is, as well as what he wishes to become. The martial artist is responsible and accountable for what he does or does not do. Some martial artists may regard the hard work that is required to attain the mental skills in this book as a sacrifice, but the highly committed martial artist doesn't look at it as a choice that involves sacrifice. He's glad to do whatever he feels can help him get what he wants.

It is my hope that you truly want to become the very best martial artist you can be. My approach to development is to ripen the total martial artist. The mental and physical skills that go into peak performance in martial arts cannot be separated from one another. It is my hope that this book will help you to refine the mental side of your approach to martial arts.

Reference

Anderson, Dave. In The Corner. New York: Morrow, 1991

Benson, Herbert. The Relaxation Response. New York: William Morrow & Co. 1975

Block, Ben Alex. The Legend Of Bruce Lee. New York: Dell Publishing Co. 1974

Durbin Sr., Bruce. Portrait of an Athlete. Illinois: Leisure Press, 1945

Garfield, A Charles, and Bennett, Zina Hal. Peak Performance. California: Warner Books, 1984

Harary,Keith. Right-Brain Learning in 30 Days. New York: St. Martins Press, 1991

Hauser, Thomas. Muhammed Ali. New York: Touchstone, 1991

Herrigel, Eugen. Zen In The Art of Archery. New York: Vintage, 1989

Loeher, E. James. Mental Toughness Training For Sports. New York: The Stephen Green Press,1982

Maltz, Maxwell. Psycho-Cybernetics. New York: Simon & Schuster, 1960

Nicklaus, Jack. Golf My Way. New York: Simon & Schuster, 1974

Nideffer, M. Robert. Athletes Guide To Mental Training. Illinois: Human Kinetics Books, 1985

Orlick, Terry. In Pursuit of Excellence. Illinois: Leisure Press, 1980

Shakti, Gawain. Creative Visualization. New York: Bantam Books, 1982

Swami, Rama and Ballentine, Rudolph M.D., Hymes, Alan M.D. <u>Science Of Breath</u>. Pennsylvania: The Himalayan Int'l Institute, 1979

Waitley, Denis. <u>The Psychology Of Winning</u>. New York: Berkeley Books, 1984